Music Discovery Book 1

Emilie Griffin

Music for Little Mozarts

Singing, Listening, Music Appreciation, Movement and Rhythm Activities to Bring Out the Music in Every Young Child

Cover illustration and interior art by Christine Finn

Christine H. Barden · Gayle Kowalchyk · E. L. Lancaster

ISBN 0-88284-967-0

Foreword

Recent studies suggest that playing and listening to music at a young age improves learning, memory, reasoning ability and general creativity. Research also supports the theory that young children who are exposed to music develop enhanced cognitive skills. The *Music for Little Mozarts* series was written to provide appropriate piano instruction for four-, five- and six-year-olds while simultaneously developing listening skills. The series was designed to provide a balance between the discipline necessary for playing the instrument and the enjoyment one gets from the process of music-making.

The course centers around the adventures of Beethoven Bear and Mozart Mouse as they learn about music. Three books guide the children through a comprehensive approach to musical learning. In the *Music Lesson Book,* students are introduced to new musical concepts and performance of pieces at the piano as they follow the story of Beethoven Bear and Mozart Mouse. Plush animals of the two characters are integral to making the course fun for young students. The *Music Workbook* contains carefully designed pages to color, that reinforce the musical concepts introduced in the Music Lesson Book. In addition, well-planned listening activities develop ear-training skills. The *Music Discovery Book* contains songs that allow the students to experience music through singing, movement and response to rhythm patterns. Music appreciation is fostered through carefully chosen music that introduces the students to great music through the ages. Melodies to sing, using either solfege or letter names, help students learn to match pitch and discover tonal elements of music. Correlated compact disc recordings for materials in the Music Lesson and Music Discovery Books are essential to achieve the goals of the course. General MIDI disks also are available for students or teachers who have the necessary equipment. A Starter Kit includes a music bag for carrying lesson materials, a music activity board and the two plush animal characters (Beethoven Bear and Mozart Mouse).

Role of Parents: The teacher serves as a musical guide for young students in fostering their curiosity, natural ability and interest, but parents also play an important role in guiding their child's musical training. The authors recommend that parents attend lessons with their child and participate actively in the learning process. Parents will need to read the directions to their child during daily practice. Regularity of practice is important; short practice sessions of 10–15 minutes are suggested for young students, with activities changing frequently within the practice time. (Teachers can give valuable suggestions regarding practice.) Patience, sincere praise and a show of enthusiasm about new materials will be very beneficial. A musical partnership between parents and child in a nurturing environment provides quality time for fostering important family relationships.

Notes to the Teacher: The course is easy to use both in private and group lessons. Through careful pacing and reinforcement, appealing music with clever lyrics is introduced in the Music Lesson Book. The Music Workbook and Music Discovery Books are correlated page by page with the Music Lesson Book to provide well-balanced lessons. A separate Teacher's Handbook offers suggestions and lesson plans to aid the teacher with planning. All books contain clean and uncluttered pages, clear music engraving and attractive artwork to complement the music and appeal to young children.

About the Music Discovery, Book 1: The Music Discovery Book reinforces each concept presented in the Music Lesson Book through singing, listening and movement. Included in the book are songs to sing for fun, motion songs to introduce musical response to music, and songs to reinforce specific rhythm patterns. The songs are a mixture of familiar folk songs and originally composed music for young children. Appealing classical music, familiar marches, and circus music are used for music appreciation activities. The music introduces students to a variety of musical styles, tempi, dynamics, moods and feelings. *Listen and Sing* pages for pitch and interval study include melodies for singing with solfege or letter names, and interesting accompaniments. The music on each page is contained on the CD and is identified by an icon that shows the track number. Students should be encouraged to listen to the music on the entire CD even before they study it in the Music Discovery Book. Music on the GM disk is also identified by an icon, followed by the Type 0 file number and the Type 1 file number (in parentheses). Each song and musical activity in the book should be studied in several subsequent lessons after its introduction.

The authors and publisher of this course offer our best wishes to children, parents and teachers as you begin this new adventure. It is certain to be richly rewarding!

Table of Contents

Hello Song 4
Activities: sing, color
Hello Song (It's Music Time Today) (song) . . .6

If You're Happy and You Know It 8
Activities: sing, trace, color
If You're Happy and You Know It (song) . . .9

Racing Car 10
Activities: sing; play glissando and clusters
Racing Car (song) .11

Clownin' Around (recording) 12
Activities: dance, color

Finger Play Song .14
Activities: sing, wiggle and tap fingers
Finger Play Song (song) 15

Hickory, Dickory, Dock! 16
Activities: sing; clap or tap rhythm
Hickory, Dickory, Dock! (song) 16

Mexican Hat Dance 18
Activities: clap, walk, sing, play rhythm instruments
Mexican Hat Dance (song) 18

Making Friends with Ludwig van Beethoven 20
Activities: draw

Ludwig van Beethoven's *Rage over the Lost Penny* (recording) . . .21
Activities: listen, clap, tap, play rhythm instruments, color

Making Friends with Wolfgang Amadeus Mozart 22
Activities: draw

Wolfgang Amadeus Mozart's *Variations on Twinkle, Twinkle, Little Star* (recording) . .23
Activities: listen; decide loud or soft, fast or slow; color

Old MacDonald Had a Farm 24
Activities: sing; play rhythm instrument or clap; find and circle three black keys, two black keys, quarter note, quarter rest
Old MacDonald Had a Farm (song) 24

Mister Elephant's Funky Dance 26
Activities: sing; clap or tap; play C's using given rhythm
Mister Elephant's Funky Dance (song) 26

John Philip Sousa's *Stars and Stripes Forever* (recording) . . .28
Activities: march; clap or tap

Listen and Sing No. 1 29
Activities: listen, sing syllables or letter names, play melody

Giant's Lullaby 30
Activities: walk; clap or tap; play A's using given rhythm
Giant's Lullaby (song) 31

Do Re Mi Tapping Song 32
Activities: sing, move
Do Re Mi Tapping Song (song) 32

Wolfgang Amadeus Mozart's Dance (recording) 34
Activities: listen, dance, color
Minuet in F Major 35

Ludwig van Beethoven's *Fifth Symphony* (recording) 36
Activities: name instruments, listen, conduct, color
Symphony No. 5 in C Minor 37

Listen and Sing No. 2 38
Activities: listen, sing syllables or letter names, play melody

Listen and Sing No. 3 39
Activities: listen, sing syllables or letter names, play melody

Twinkle, Twinkle, Little Star 40
Activities: sing; clap or tap; play rhythm instruments
Twinkle, Twinkle, Little Star (song) 40

Listen and Sing No. 4 42
Activities: listen, sing syllables or letter names, play melody

Put the Beat in Your Feet 43
Activities: sing, move
Put the Beat in Your Feet (song) 44

Listen and Sing No. 5 46
Activities: listen, sing syllables or letter names, play melody

Listen and Sing No. 6 47
Activities: listen, sing syllables or letter names, play melody

Goodbye Song 48
Activity: sing
It's Time to Say Goodbye (song) 48

Use with Alfred's Music for Little Mozarts,
Lesson Book 1, page 4.

Hello Song

(It's Music Time Today)

Sing the *Hello Song* (pages 6–7) with Mozart Mouse, Beethoven Bear, your teacher and your music friends as you begin each lesson.

Use with page 4.

Mozart Mouse and Beethoven Bear have such fun singing and moving to music. Color their pictures as you sing or listen to the *Hello Song*.

Use with page 4 and at the beginning of every lesson.

Hello Song
(It's Music Time Today)

1 1 (21)

Christine H. Barden

*After the first few lessons, you may begin the *Hello Song* here if so desired.

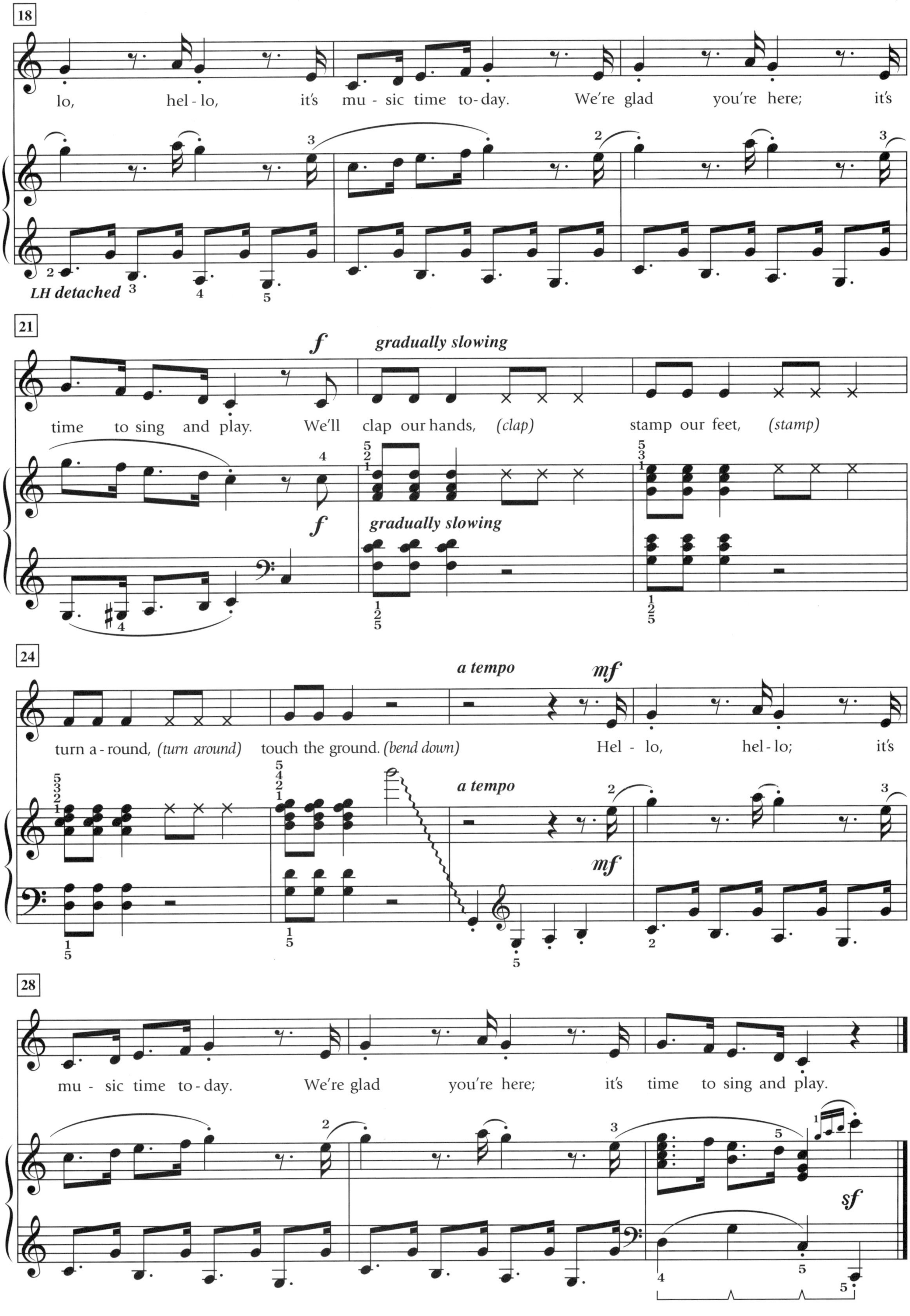
18
lo, hel - lo, it's mu - sic time to - day. We're glad you're here; it's
LH detached
21
f
gradually slowing
time to sing and play. We'll clap our hands, (clap) stamp our feet, (stamp)
f
gradually slowing
24
a tempo
mf
turn a - round, (turn around) touch the ground. (bend down) Hel - lo, hel - lo; it's
a tempo
mf
28
mu - sic time to - day. We're glad you're here; it's time to sing and play.
sf

Use with page 7.

If You're Happy and You Know It

Music makes Beethoven Bear and Mozart Mouse *very* happy.

1. Sing *If You're Happy and You Know It,* doing the motions suggested in the words.
2. Trace the smile on the face of Beethoven Bear and Mozart Mouse.
3. Color the picture.

Use with page 7.

If You're Happy and You Know It

2 2(22)

arr. Christine H. Barden

5

hap-py and you know it clap your hands! *(clap hands)* If you're hap-py and you know it, then your

8

face will sure-ly show it, If you're hap-py and you know it, clap your hands! *(clap hands)*

2. stamp your feet *(stamp feet)*

3. jump up high *(jump high)*
*Teacher plays white key glissando going up and down on the two beats of rest.

4. do all three *(clap hands, stamp feet, jump high)*

5. Other options: play up high ( ), play down low ( )

Use with page 9.

Racing Car

Beethoven Bear and Mozart Mouse want *you* to drive a racing car.

1. Pretend that you are in the driver's seat as you sing *Racing Car.*
2. Sing again and play a glissando each time you say "zoom." Honk your horn by tapping "beep, beep, beep" on black keys.

Racing Car

Use with page 9.

① Student plays a white key glissando beginning and ending on any key.

② Student plays a group of black keys (cluster) in this rhythm.

Use with page 11.

Clowning' Around

Let's go to the circus with Beethoven Bear and Mozart Mouse.

1. Do a funny dance with the clowns and with your music friends as you listen to the recording.
2. Color the picture of the circus, as you listen to the recording again.

Use with page 13.

Finger Play Song

Practice your finger numbers with Beethoven Bear and Mozart Mouse.

1. Sing the *Finger Play Song.* Hold both hands up with fingers open wide; wiggle each finger as you sing about it.
2. Keeping your hands open wide, tap each finger on the picture below as you sing the song again.

Use with page 13.

Finger Play Song*

arr. Christine H. Barden

2. Pointer is finger number 2. . . .
3. Tall Man is finger number 3. . . .
4. Ring Man is finger number 4. . . .
5. Pinky is finger number 5. . . .

* For a variation on the words, sing: "Where is finger number one, etc.?" As students become comfortable with identifying numbers, ask them to show fingers in a random order.

Use with page 17.

Hickory, Dickory, Dock!

The "tick tock tick tock" sounds of the clock in the music room remind Beethoven Bear and Mozart Mouse to keep a steady beat.

1. Sing *Hickory, Dickory, Dock,* swinging your arms with a steady "tick tock tick tock" motion.
2. Sing again, and clap or tap the rhythm pattern below.

♩ ♩ ♩ ♩

arr. Christine H. Barden

Note to Teacher: Play this piece with a feeling of 2 beats per measure. Students should clap a quarter note for each pulse. (A quarter note in the student rhythm pattern equals a dotted quarter note in the song.)

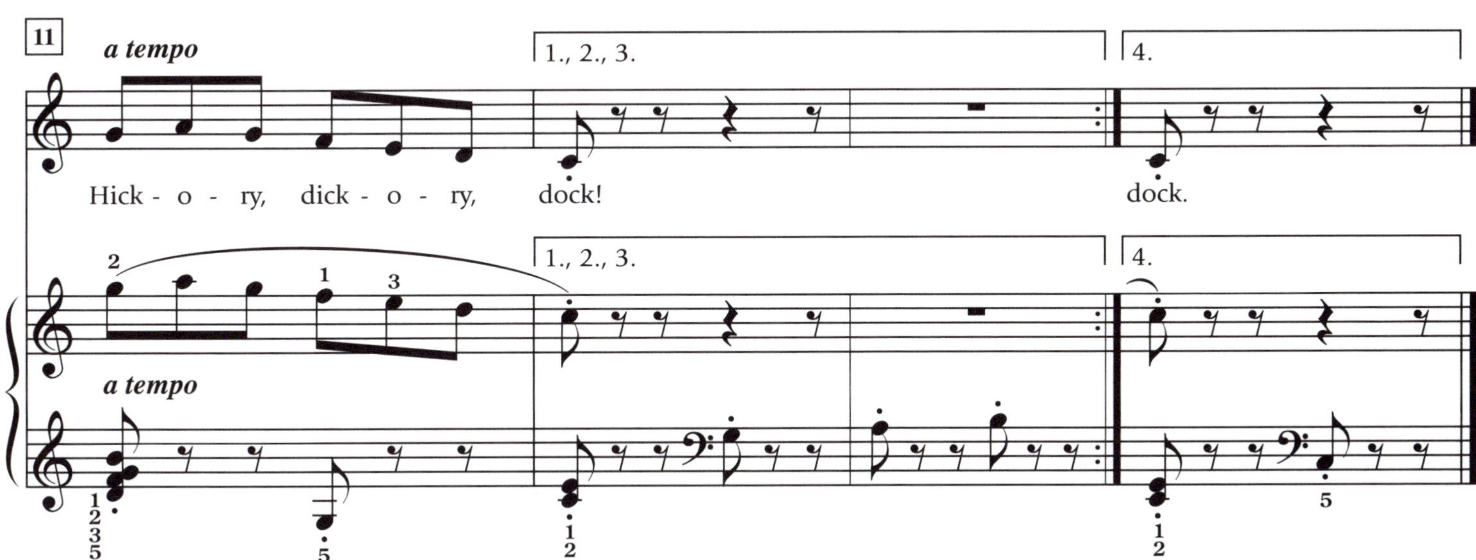

Additional words by Christine H. Barden

2. Hickory, dickory, dee!
The mouse ran up a tree.
Oh, please come down and play with me.
Hickory, dickory, dee!

3. Hickory, dickory, doo!
The mouse is in my shoe.
His little nose is tickling my toes.
Hickory, dickory, doo!

4. Hickory, dickory, day!
The mouse has run away.
I hope that he'll come back to play.
Hickory, dickory, day!

* *Optional:* Students can play the following on the piano for the remainder of the piece: E D C

Mexican Hat Dance

Use with page 19.

1. Sing *Mexican Hat Dance,* doing the motions suggested in the song. In the section without words, clap a steady beat or walk in a circle.
2. Sing again and play rhythm instruments to keep a steady beat.

arr. Christine H. Barden

9
4th time to Coda
1.
clap, we clap, we clap, then stop and take a rest. (shh!) We
4th time to Coda
1.
13
2.
rest.
2.
f
17
21
1.
2.
D. S. al Coda
We
1.
2.
D. S. al Coda
mf
Coda
rest. (shh!)
8va

Use with page 20.

Making Friends with Ludwig van Beethoven

Beethoven Bear was named after his mother's favorite composer, Ludwig van Beethoven.

Ludwig van Beethoven was born in Bonn, Germany, in 1770—around the time that trains were invented. At this time, there was no electricity, cars or telephones. He started piano lessons with his father when he was four years old. When he was 17 he played for Wolfgang Amadeus Mozart in Vienna. Beethoven wrote music for orchestra, chorus, piano and other instruments. He is known as a Classical-Romantic composer since his music serves as a bridge between the two periods.

Draw or paste a picture of yourself next to Ludwig van Beethoven in the Gallery of Famous Musicians.

Use with page 20.

Ludwig van Beethoven's *Rage over the Lost Penny*

8

Ludwig van Beethoven wrote many compositions for piano including variations, dances, short pieces and 32 longer works called sonatas. One of his most famous compositions is the *Rage over the Lost Penny.*

1. Listen to this piece and tap the rhythm below during the soft (***p***) sections. Clap the same rhythm during the loud (***f***) sections.

2. Listen to the music again using bells for the rhythm during the soft (***p***) sections, and a tambourine for the rhythm during the loud (***f***) sections.
3. Listen to the music a third time and color the picture of Beethoven looking for his lost penny.

Use with page 21.

Making Friends with Wolfgang Amadeus Mozart

Wolfgang Amadeus Mozart was a favorite composer of the Mouse family.

Wolfgang Amadeus Mozart was born in Salzburg, Austria, in 1756 a few years before Ludwig van Beethoven was born. Like Ludwig van Beethoven, he began studying keyboard with his father when he was four years old. Mozart often played duets with his sister, Nannerl.

He is an important composer from the Classical Period. Not unlike Mozart Mouse, Wolfgang was a fun-loving person and liked to play jokes on people. He wrote many compositions, including operas, symphonies and piano music.

Draw or paste a picture of yourself next to Wolfgang Amadeus Mozart in the Gallery of Famous Musicians.

Use with page 21.

Wolfgang Amadeus Mozart's *Variations on Twinkle, Twinkle, Little Star*

Like Beethoven, Wolfgang Amadeus Mozart also wrote many works for piano including sonatas, variations and dances. One of Wolfgang Amadeus Mozart's most famous compositions for piano is the *Variations on Twinkle, Twinkle, Little Star (Ah, vous dirai-je, Maman)*. Mozart created variations by changing the music or adding things to it.

1. Listen to the theme and four variations and decide if they are:
   - loud or soft
   - fast or slow
2. Listen to the music again and color the picture of Mozart looking at the stars.

Use with page 22.

Old MacDonald Had a Farm

1. Sing *Old MacDonald Had a Farm.*
   Play a rhythm instrument or clap on each *E-I-E-I-O.*
2. Some musical symbols are hiding in Old MacDonald's Farm.
   Find and circle the following as you listen to the music.
   a. a group of three black keys
   b. a group of two black keys
   c. a quarter note
   d. a quarter rest

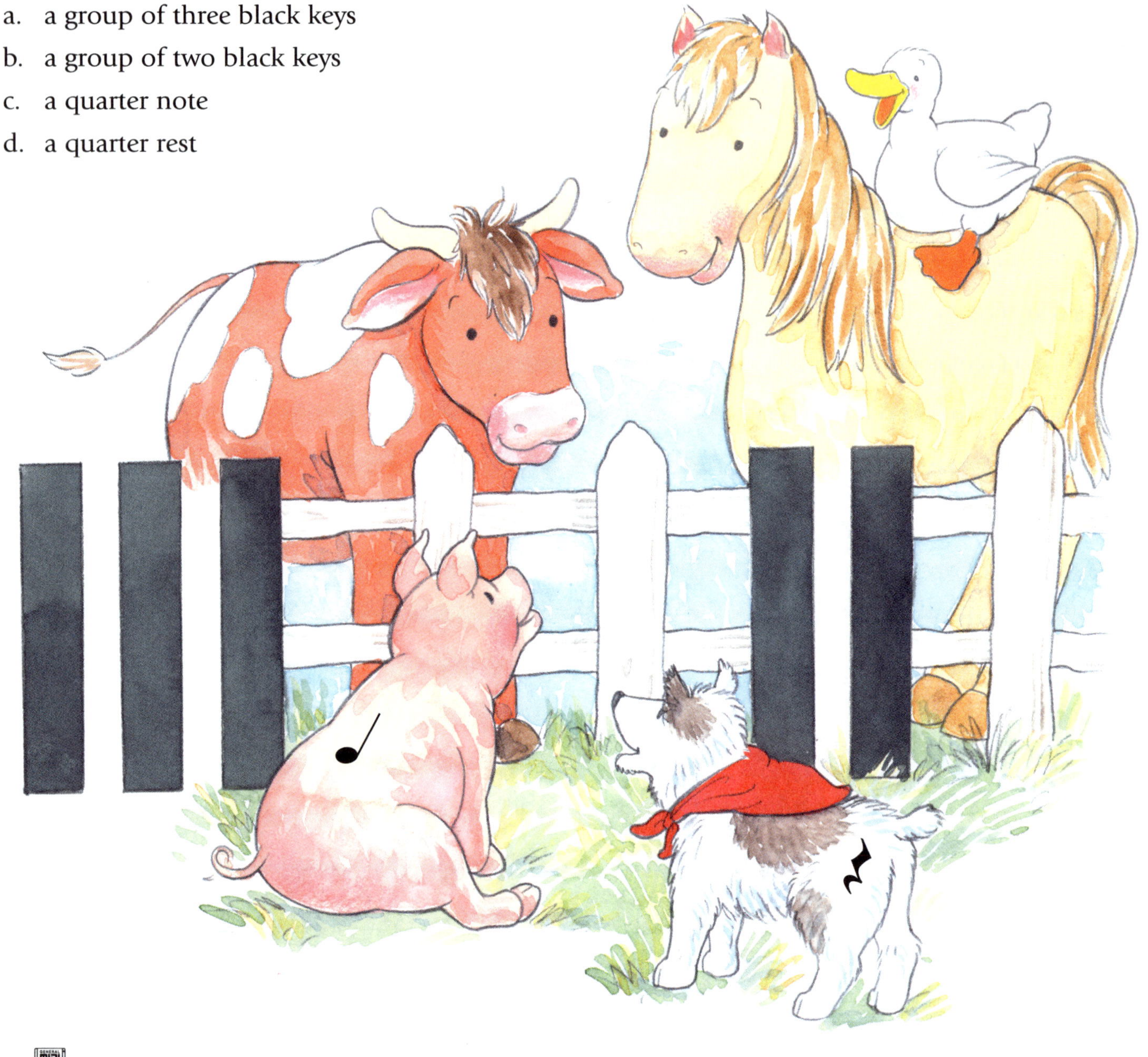

10 7 (27)

arr. Christine H. Barden

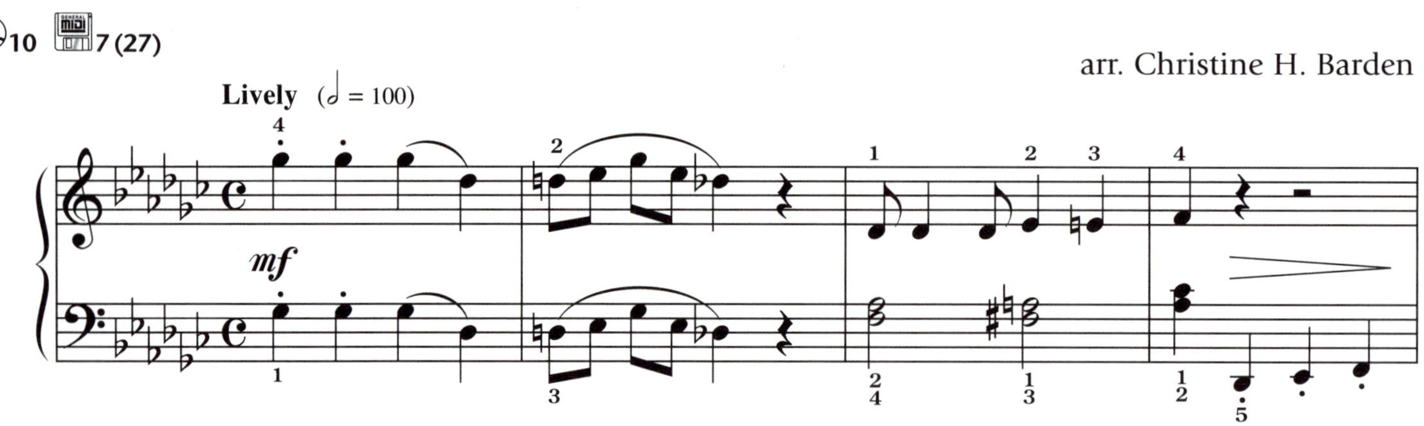

Sing the entire song using different animals:
2. cow (moo, moo)
3. pig (oink, oink)
4. horse (neigh, neigh)
5. dog (ruff, ruff)

Mister Elephant's Funky Dance

Use with page 25.

Elgar E. Elephant, a friend from the Music Room, taught Beethoven Bear and Mozart Mouse a Funky Dance.

1. Sing *Mister Elephant's Funky Dance* as an echo song.
2. Sing again and clap or tap the rhythm pattern on the banner.
3. After you have learned C on the keyboard (Music Lesson Book, page 28), review this piece. Play C's anywhere on the keyboard as you listen to the music, using the rhythm pattern on the banner.

11 8 (28)

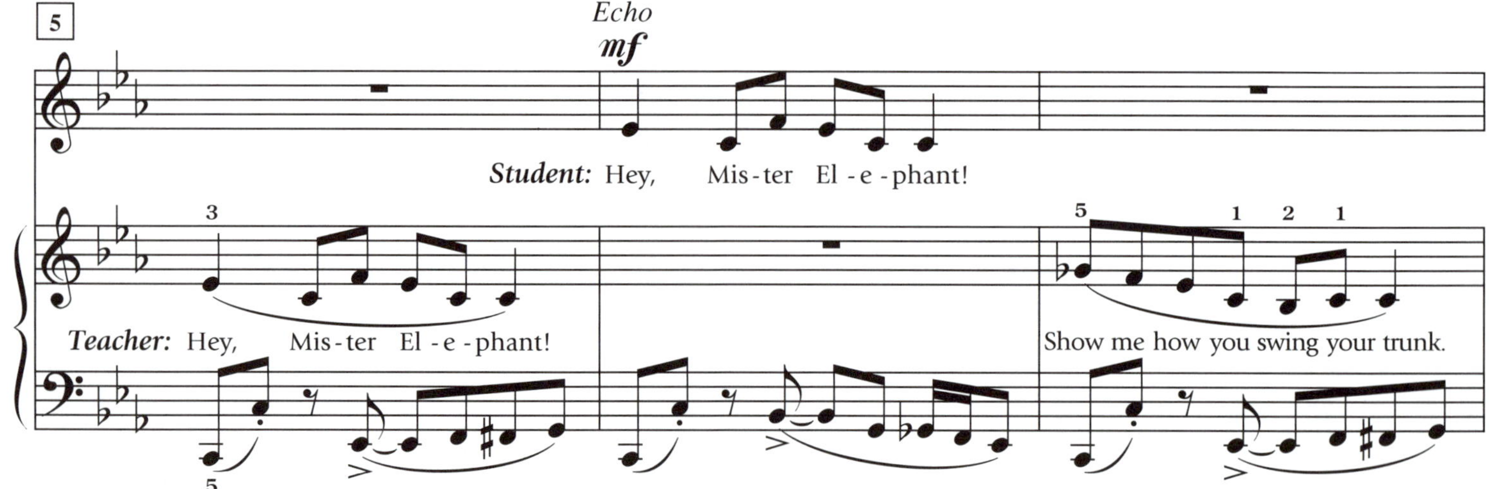

8
Show me how you swing your trunk.
Hey, Mis - ter El - e - phant!
Hey, Mis - ter El - e - phant!
11
Show me how you swing your trunk.
Flap your ears!
Show me how you swing your trunk.
Flap your ears!
14
Swish your tail!
Hey, Mis - ter El - e - phant!
Swish your tail!
Hey, Mis - ter El - e - phant!
17
Show me how you swing your trunk.
Please!
subito p
Show me how you swing your trunk.
Please!
subito p
8va

Use with page 28.

John Philip Sousa's *Stars and Stripes Forever*

12

John Philip Sousa is an American composer who was known as the "March King" since he wrote over 100 marches. He was born in 1854 in Washington, D. C., and lived after Wolfgang Amadeus Mozart and Ludwig van Beethoven. A movie was made about his life. The movie was named *Stars and Stripes Forever* after his most famous march.

1. March with your music friends as you listen to the recording of *Stars and Stripes Forever.* Take turns playing the bass drum and cymbals, leading the band and waving the flag.
2. Listen to the music again and clap or tap the rhythm pattern on the flag.

Use with page 30.

Listen and Sing No. 1

Beethoven Bear and Mozart Mouse know that listening and singing help their fingers learn to play.

1. Listen to your teacher or the recording first, then sing the melody, using syllables or letter names.
2. You may also play the melody on your piano.

Teacher Accompaniment

Christine H. Barden

Use with page 31.

Giant's Lullaby

Our music friends are getting sleepy. They ask the friendly giant to carry them.

1. Pretend to be a giant and carry Beethoven Bear and Mozart Mouse as you sing *Giant's Lullaby* and walk with giant steps.
2. Sing it again and clap or tap the rhythm pattern below.
3. After you have learned A on the keyboard (Music Lesson Book, page 42), review this piece. Play A's anywhere on the keyboard as you listen to the music, using the rhythm pattern below.

𝅗𝅥 𝅗𝅥

Use with page 31.

Giant's Lullaby

14 10 (30)

Christine H. Barden

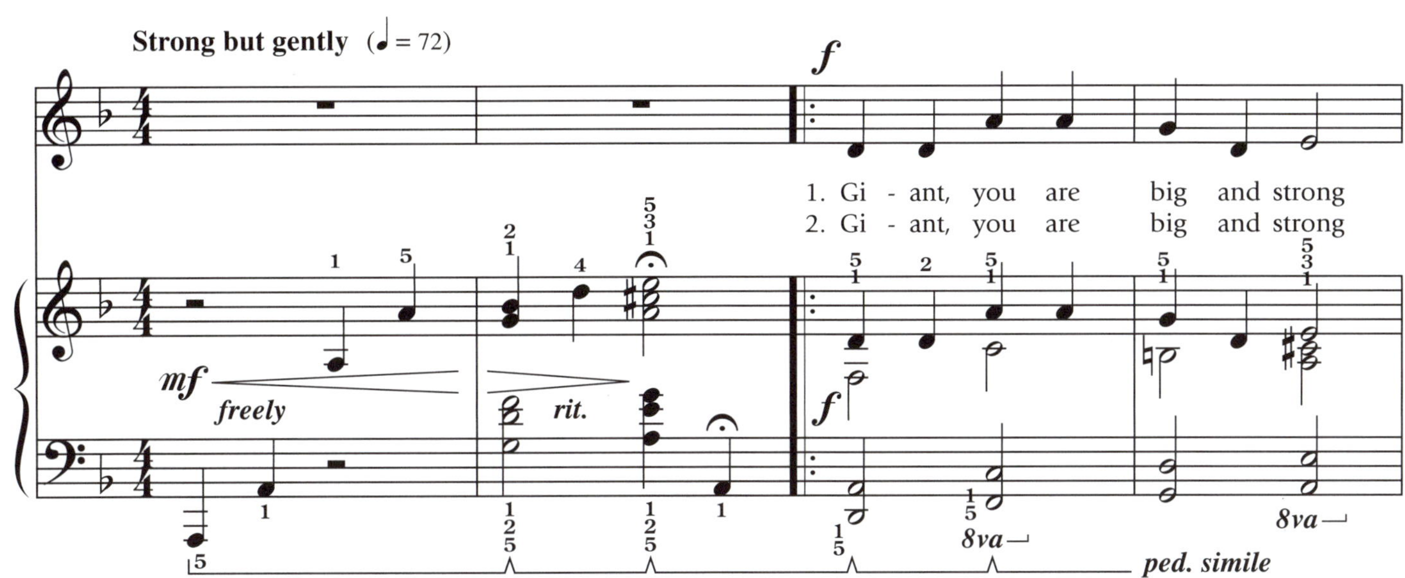

Use with page 33.

Do Re Mi Tapping Song*

Sing the *Do Re Mi Tapping Song* as an echo song, doing the motions suggested in the words.

Christine H. Barden

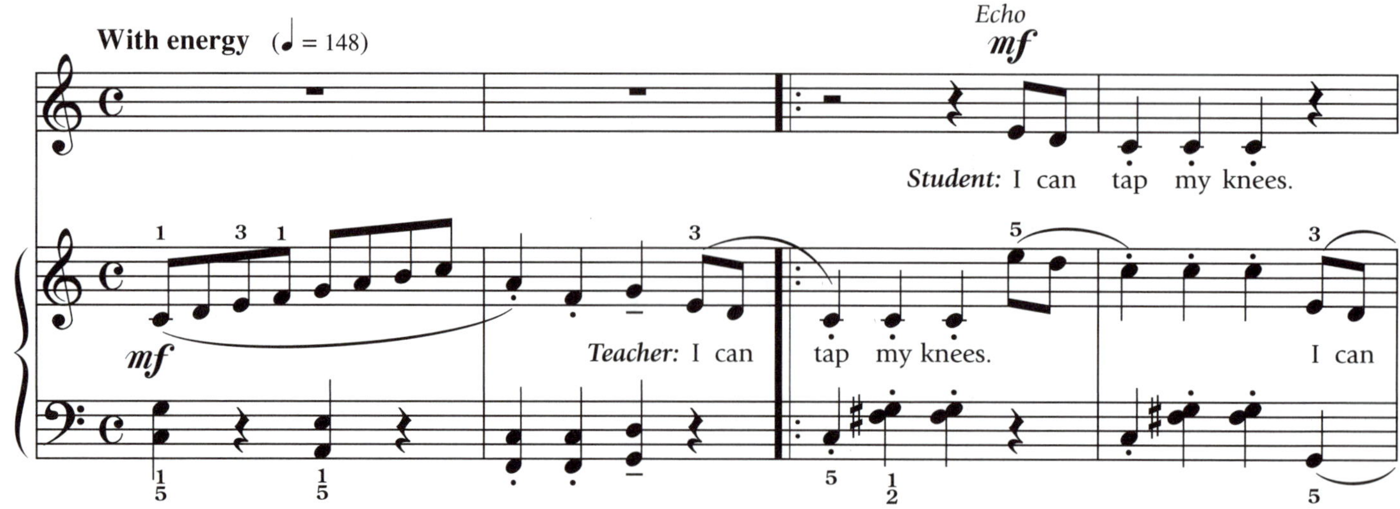

*Teacher: You can substitute C for *do*, D for *re* and E for *mi* throughout the entire piece if so desired.

*Optional: ***2nd time, accelerando poco a poco to the end.***

Use with page 34.

Wolfgang Amadeus Mozart's Dance

The minuet, a French dance, was very popular during Wolfgang Amadeus Mozart's time. Although the minuet started before Mozart was born, it continued to be danced throughout his lifetime. Mozart included minuets in many of his musical compositions. This *Minuet in F Major* for piano, was written in 1762 when he was only six years old.

1. Form a circle with your friends and dance the minuet, following the motions in the music.
2. Listen to the music again and color the picture of the dancers.

Use with page 34.

Minuet in F Major

16 12 (32)

Wolfgang Amadeus Mozart
(1756–1791)
K. 2

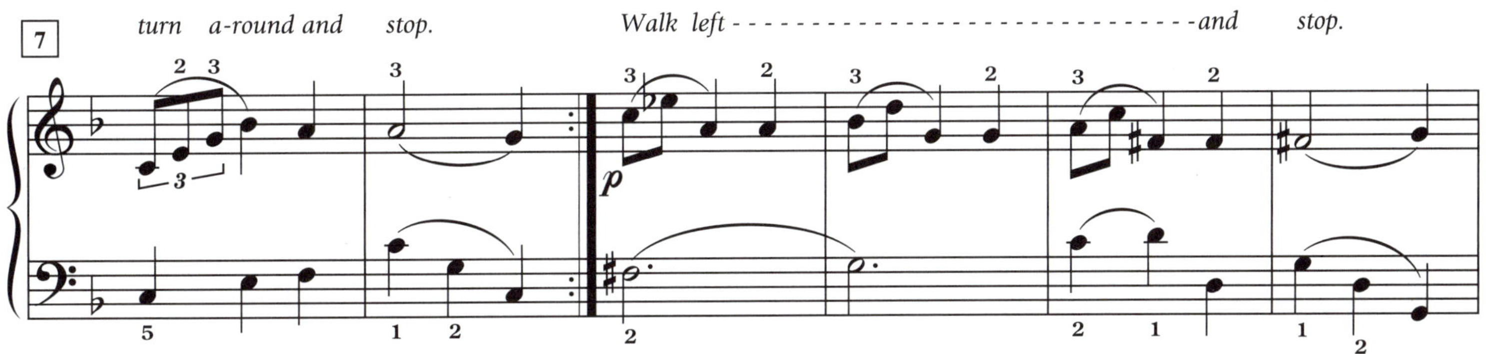

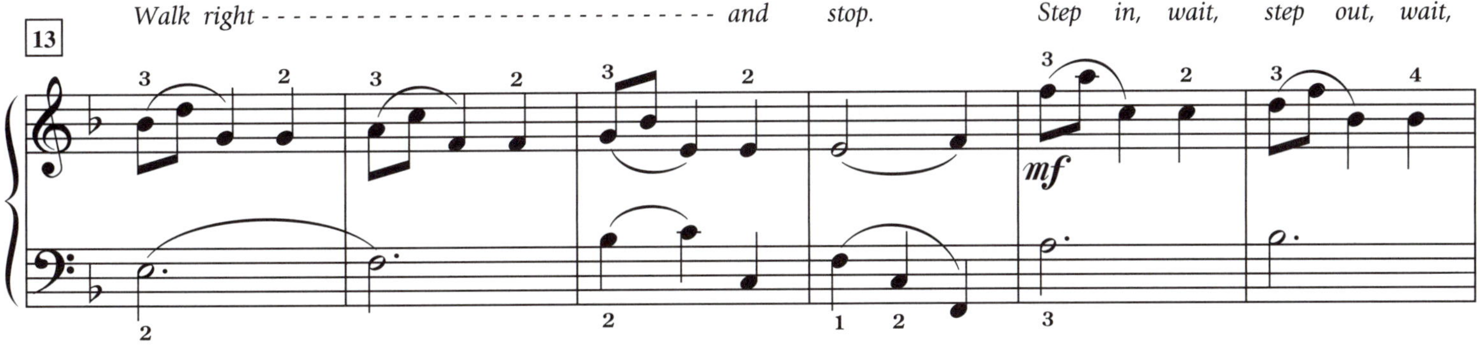

*Motions to dance *Minuet in F Major*.

Use with page 35.

Ludwig van Beethoven's *Fifth Symphony*

A symphony is a big composition written for an orchestra. The orchestra includes many different instruments. Ludwig van Beethoven wrote nine symphonies that are very important musical works. His *Fifth Symphony* is the most famous. Orchestras usually have a conductor when they play symphonies. The conductor gives cues to the orchestra with the arms and hands to help keep the musicians together during the performance.

1. Listen to Beethoven's *Fifth Symphony* and color the instruments in the picture the following colors:
   flute: silver — clarinet: black
   trombone: gold — violin: brown
2. Look at the first page of the music from Beethoven's *Fifth Symphony* on page 37 and name as many instruments as you can that are shown beside the music.

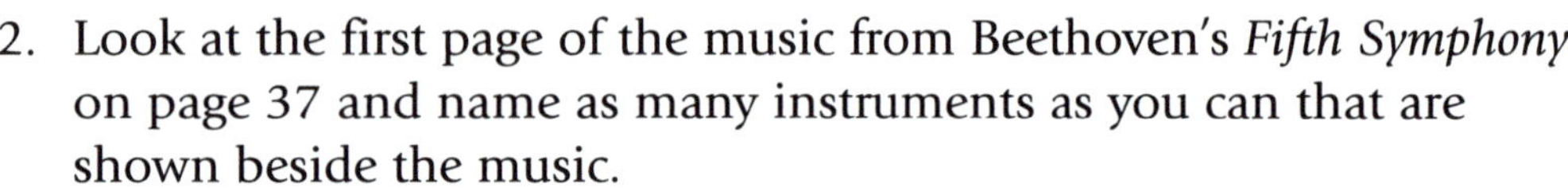

3. Listen to the music again and pretend to be a famous conductor or play your favorite instrument from the orchestra.

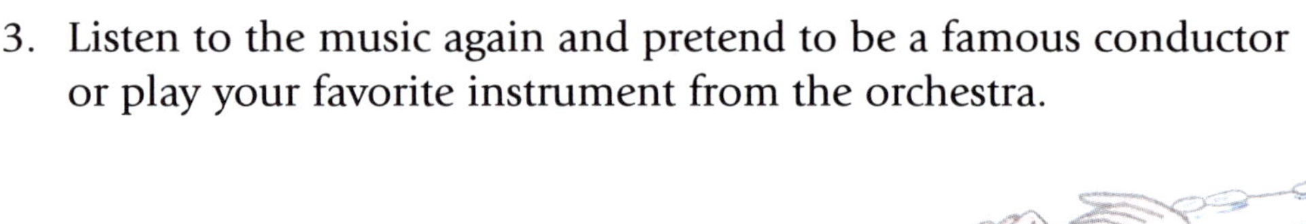

Symphony No. 5 in C Minor

17

Ludwig van Beethoven
(1770–1827)
Op. 67

Use with page 36.

Listen and Sing No. 2

1. Listen to your teacher or the recording first, then sing the melody, using syllables or letter names.
2. You may also play the melody on your piano.

C
D
E
E
D
C
Do
Re
Mi
Mi
Re
Do

Mi

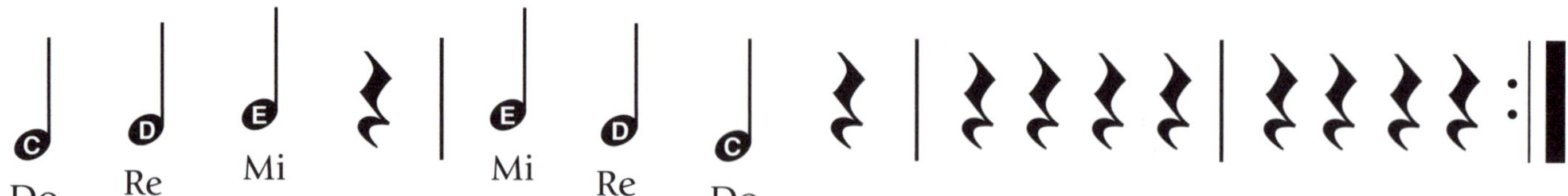

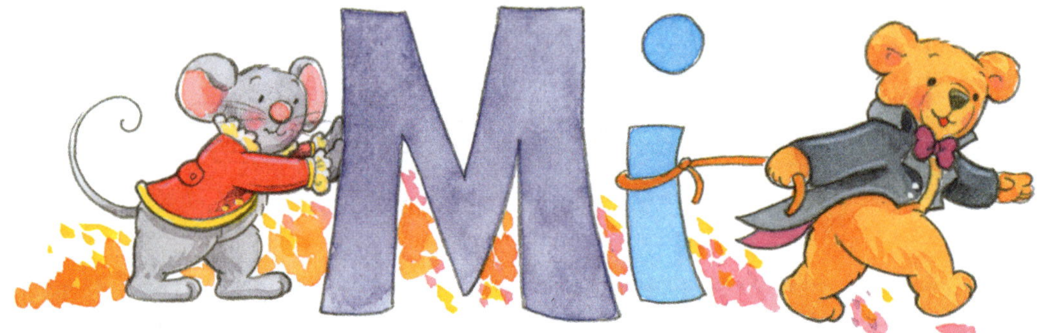

Teacher Accompaniment

18 13 (33)

Christine H. Barden

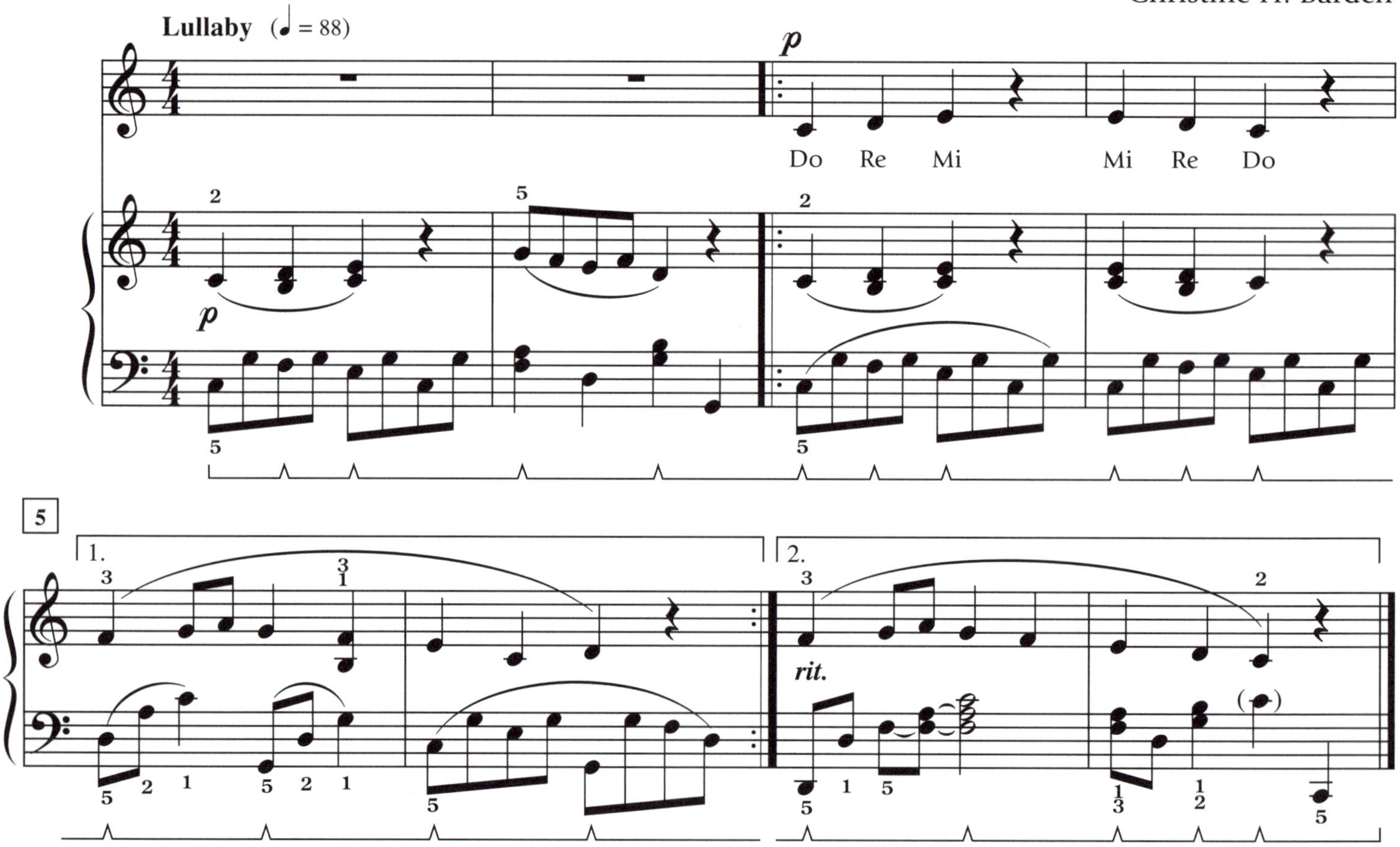
Lullaby (♩ = 88)
p
Do Re Mi
Mi Re Do
5
1.
2.
rit.

Use with page 39.

Listen and Sing No. 3

1. Listen to your teacher or the recording first, then sing the melody, using syllables or letter names.
2. You may also play the melody on your piano.

C C C
Do Do Do
B B B
Ti Ti Ti
C C B B
Do Do Ti Ti
C D E
Do Re Mi

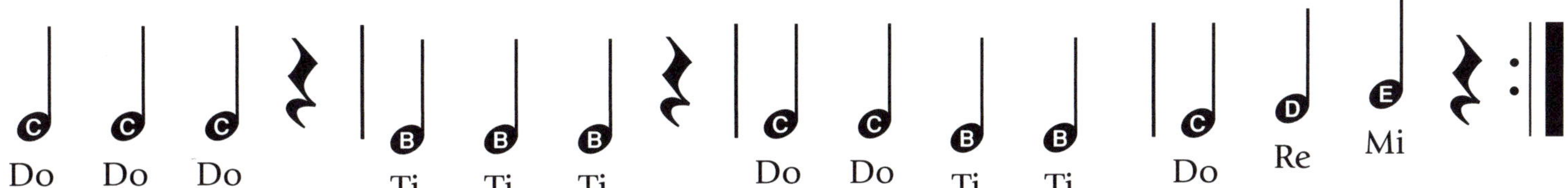

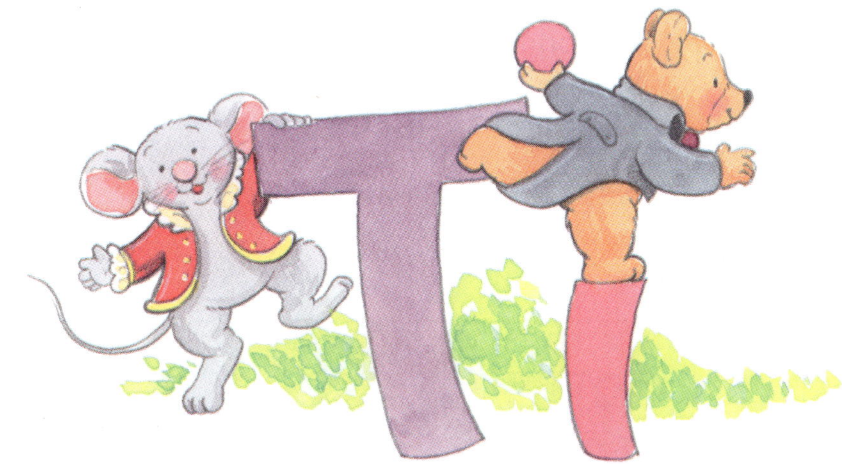

Teacher Accompaniment

19 14 (34)

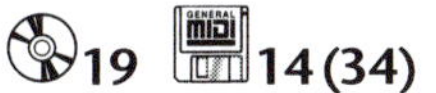

Christine H. Barden

With energy (♩ = 130)
mf
Do Do Do
mf
4
Ti Ti Ti
Do Do Ti Ti
1.
Do Re Mi
2.
Do Re Mi
rit.

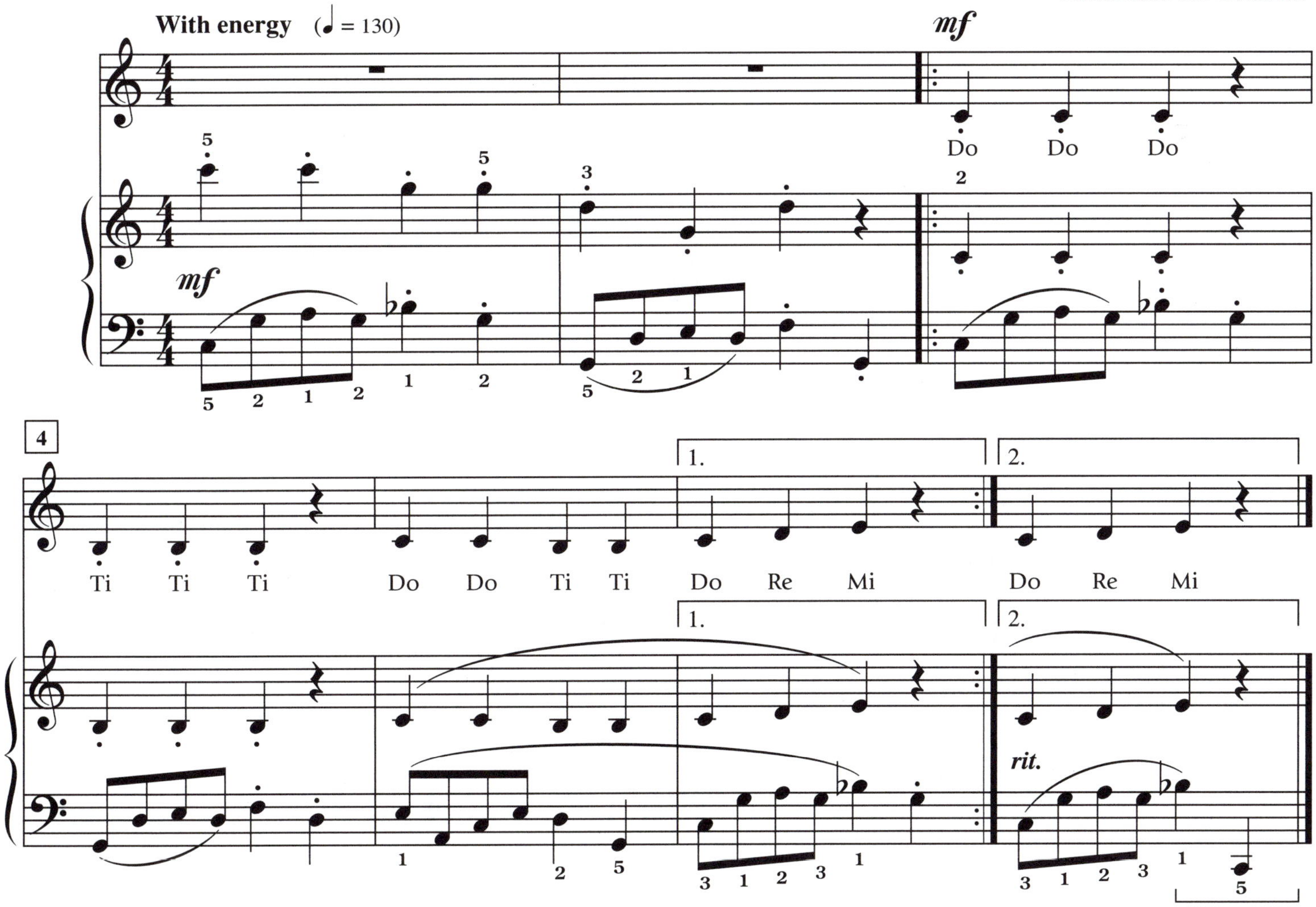

Use with page 41.

Twinkle, Twinkle, Little Star

The twinkling stars in the sky at night remind Beethoven Bear and Mozart Mouse of one of their favorite songs, *Twinkle, Twinkle, Little Star.*

1. Sing *Twinkle, Twinkle, Little Star,* clapping or tapping the following rhythm pattern:

2. Sing again and shake bells or a tambourine, using the following rhythm pattern when you sing, "Up above the world so high, like a diamond in the sky."

20 15(35)

arr. Christine H. Barden

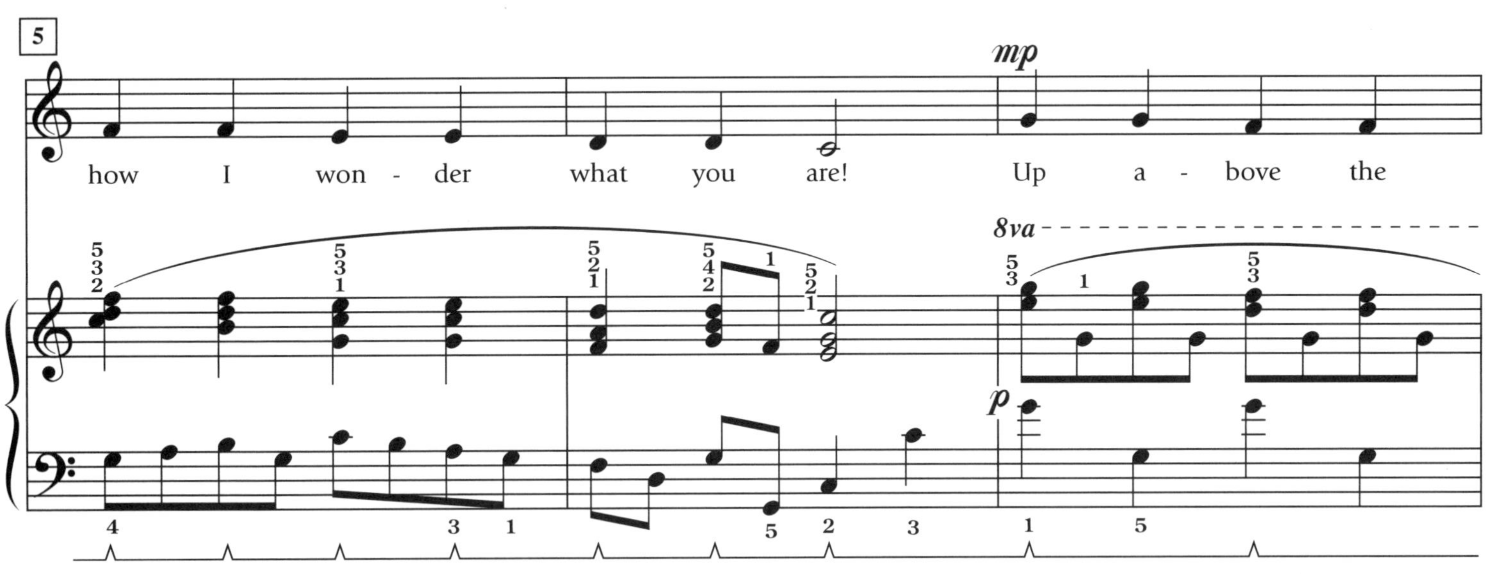
5
mp
how I won - der what you are! Up a - bove the
8va
p

8
world so high, like a dia - mond in the sky.
rit.

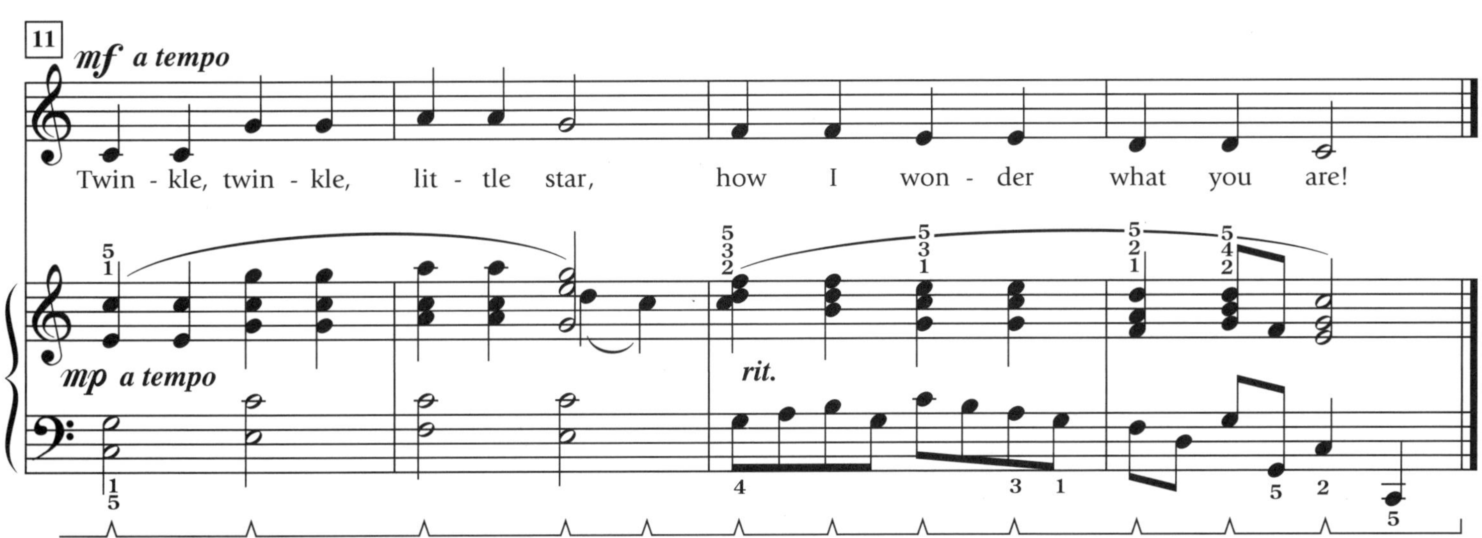
11
mf a tempo
Twin - kle, twin - kle, lit - tle star, how I won - der what you are!
mp a tempo
rit.

Listen and Sing No. 4

Use with page 43.

1. Listen to your teacher or the recording first, then sing the melody, using syllables or letter names.
2. You may also play the melody on your piano.

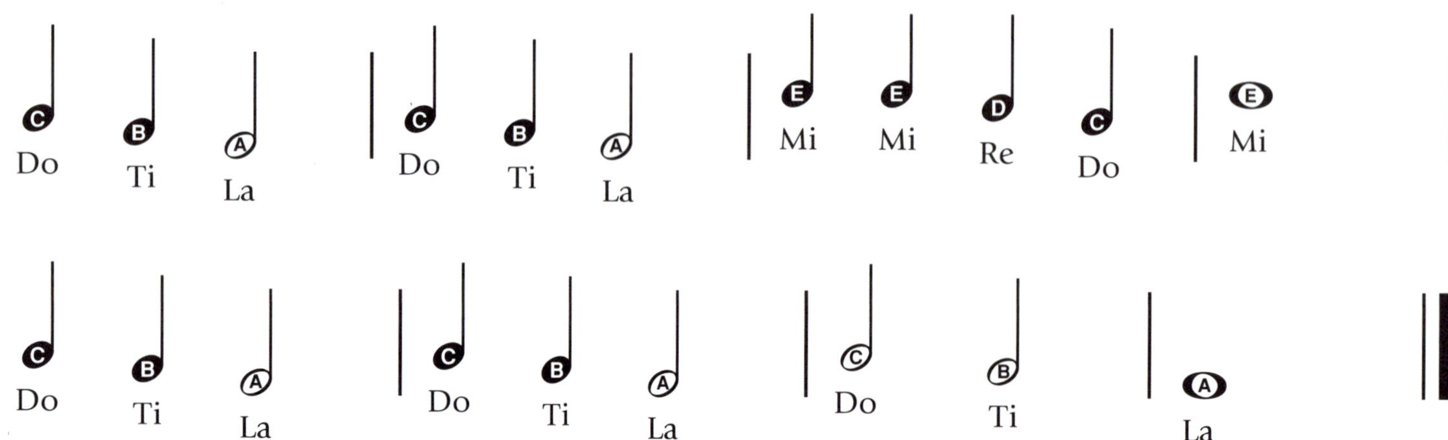

Teacher Accompaniment

Use with page 45.

Put the Beat in Your Feet

Beethoven Bear and Mozart Mouse like to play a game with this song. They walk and keep a steady beat with the music; then they stand very still when they hear *"freeze 1 - 2 - 3."* Join them and put the beat in *your feet!*

Sing *Put the Beat in Your Feet,* doing the motions suggested in the words.

Use with page 45.

Put the Beat in Your Feet

22 17 (37)

Christine H. Barden

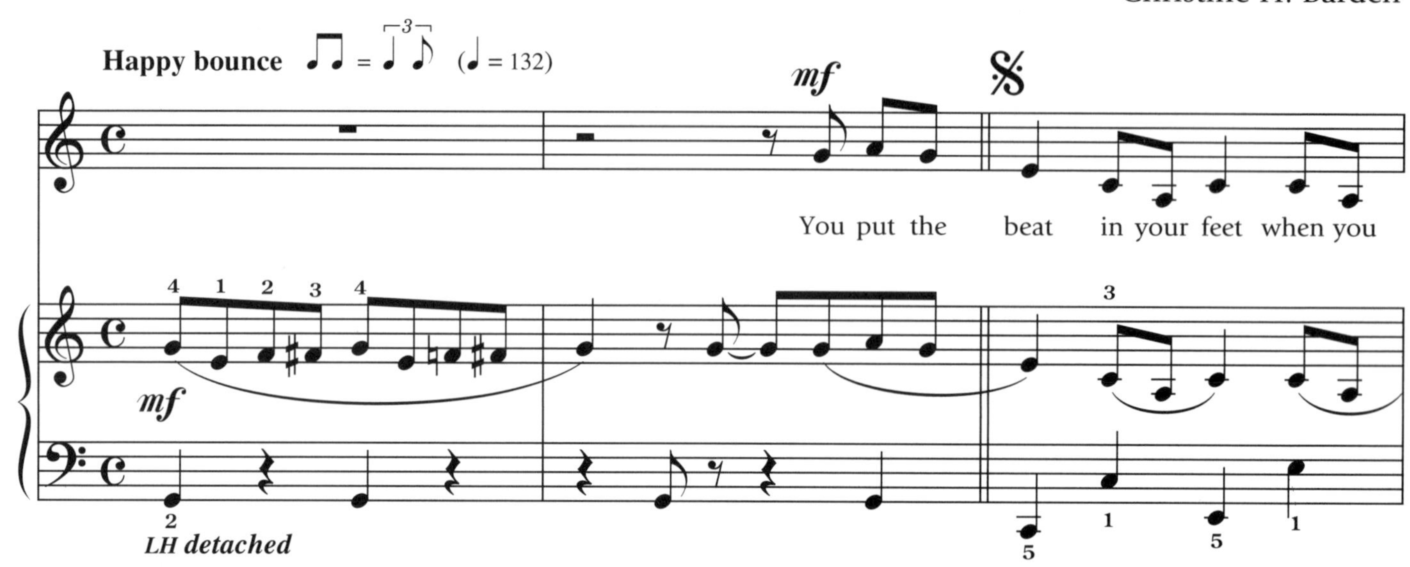

11
to Coda
walk, and walk, and walk, and stop. And then you clap your hands.
to Coda
f
f
14
Turn a-round, and then touch the ground. Feel the rhy-thm and
17
clap your hands. Then you do a lit-tle hop, hop,
20
D. S. al Coda
hop, hop, hop. You put the
D. S. al Coda
Coda
subito p
walk and you stop. Yeah!
subito p
trem.
8va

Listen and Sing No. 5

Use with page 46.

La
Ti
Do
Re
Mi

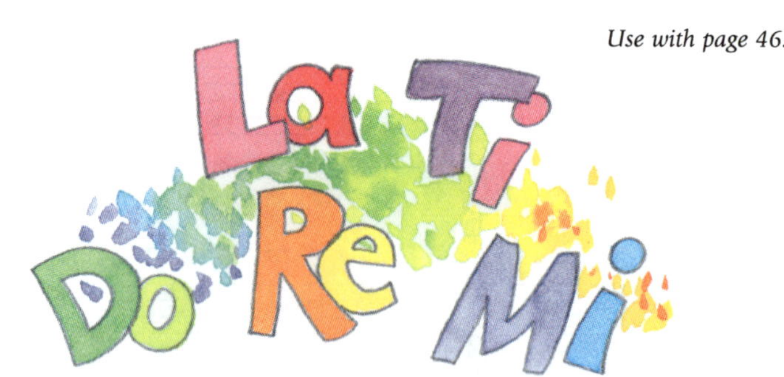

1. Listen to your teacher or the recording first, then sing the melody, using syllables or letter names.
2. You may also play the melody on your piano.

C C C A A A B B A B C D E
Do Do Do La La La Ti Ti La Ti Do Re Mi
C C C A A A B B A B C C C
Do Do Do La La La Ti Ti La Ti Do Do Do

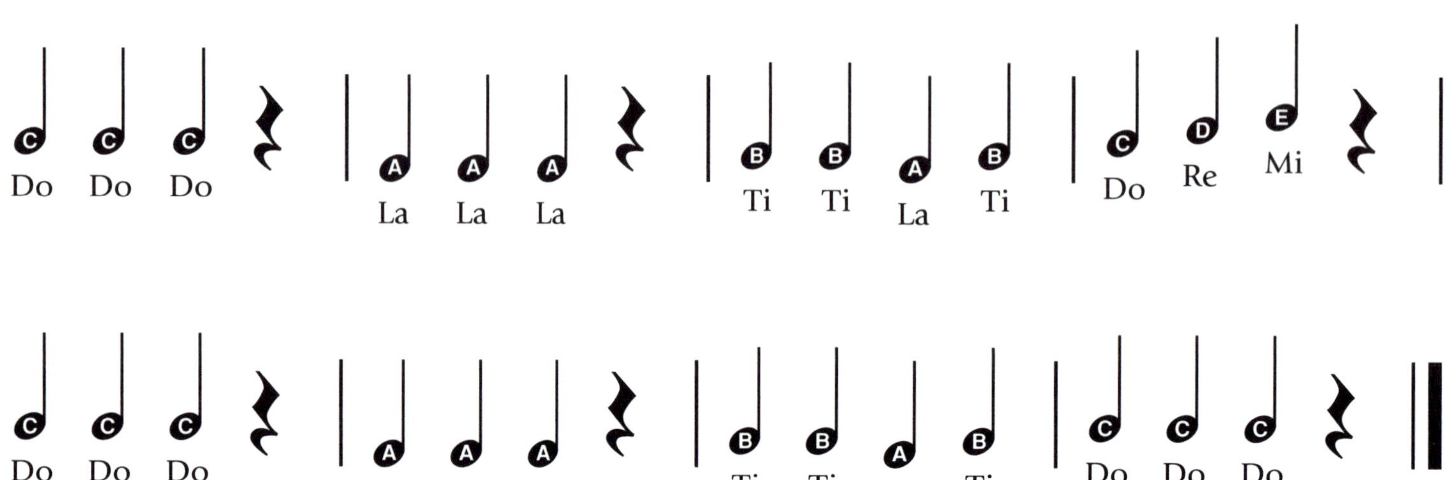

Teacher Accompaniment

23 18 (38)

Christine H. Barden

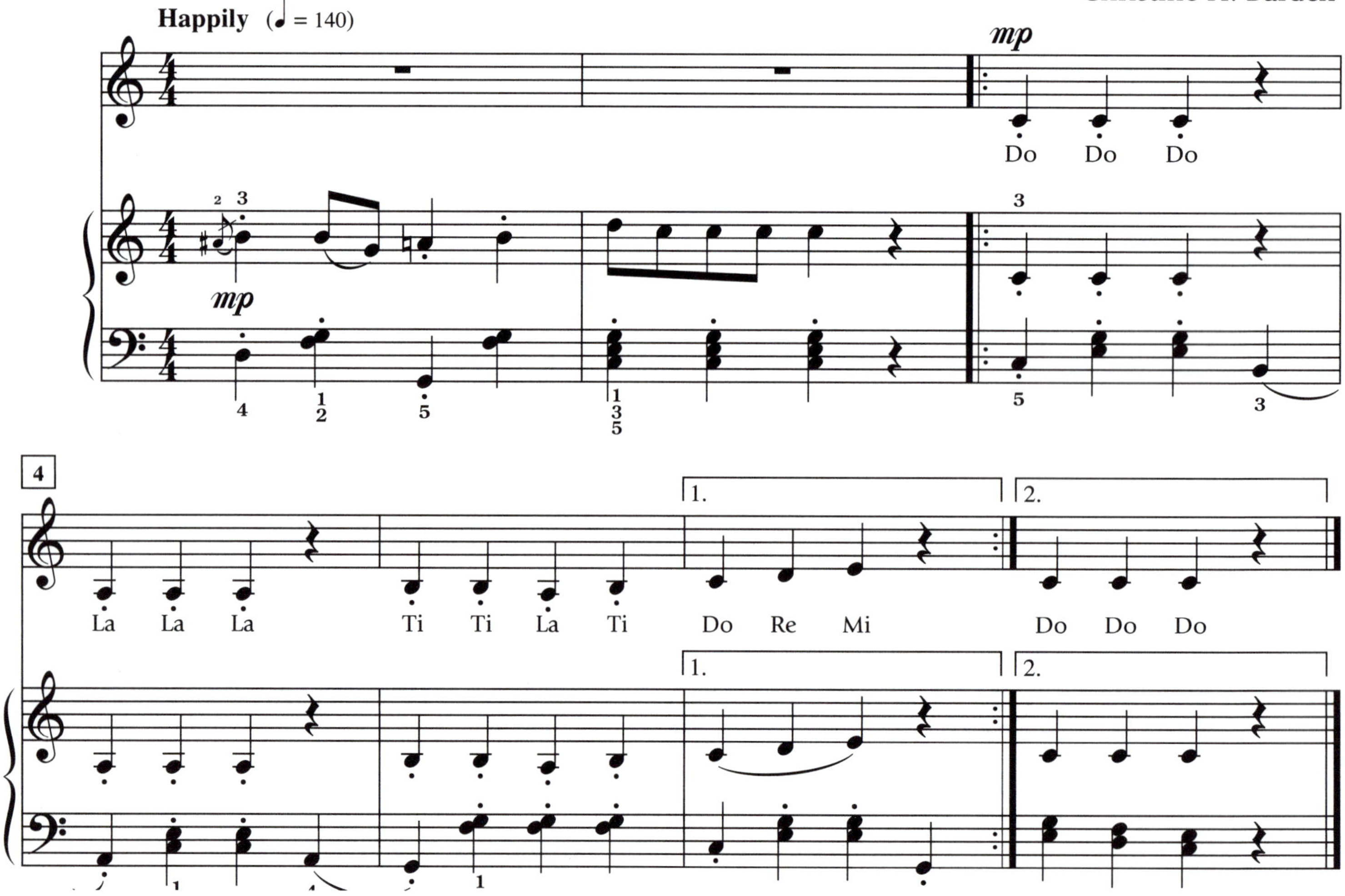

Happily (♩ = 140)
mp
Do Do Do
mp
4
La La La Ti Ti La Ti Do Re Mi Do Do Do
1.
2.

Use with page 47.

Listen and Sing No. 6

1. Listen to your teacher or the recording first, then sing the melody, using syllables or letter names.
2. You may also play the melody on your piano.

D D C D D E
Re Re Do Re Re Mi

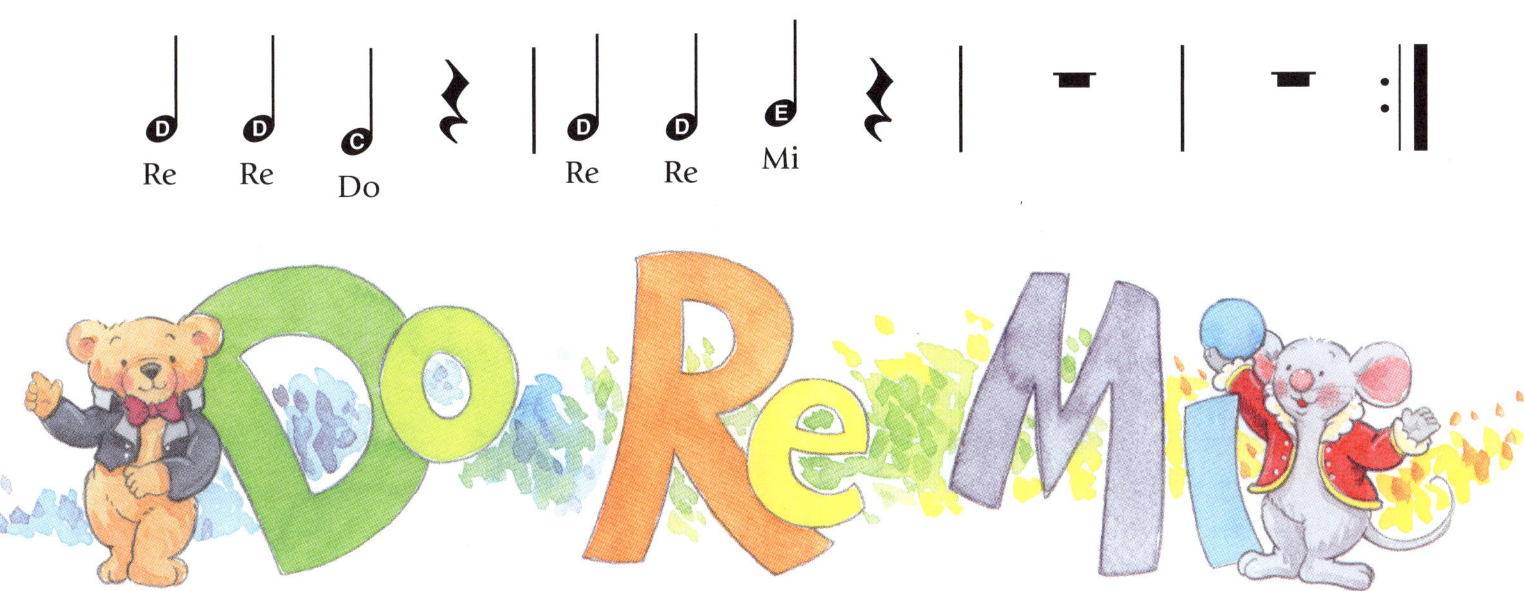

Teacher Accompaniment

24 19 (39)

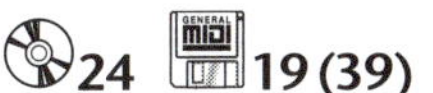

Christine H. Barden

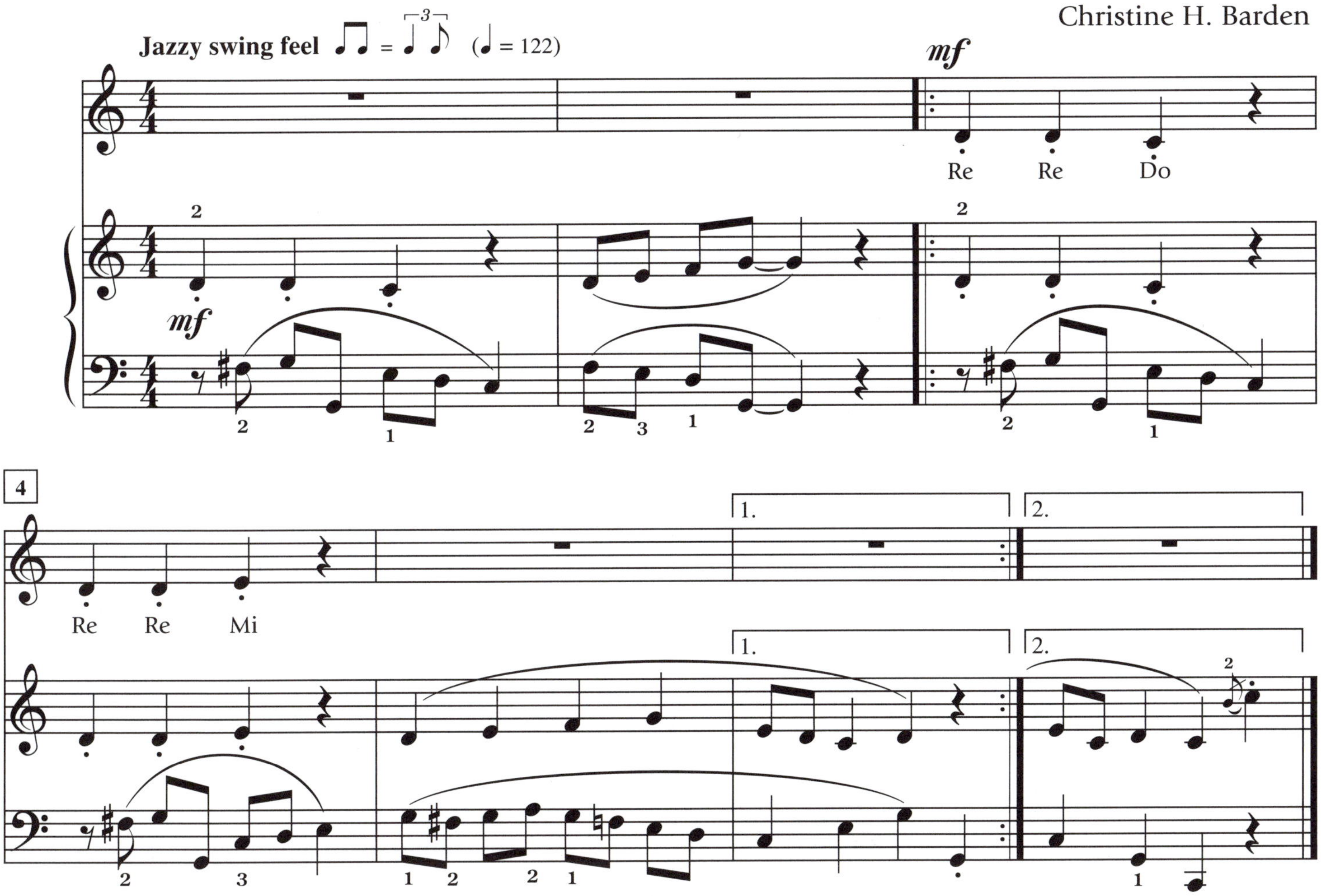
Jazzy swing feel
(♩ = 122)
mf
Re Re Do
4
Re Re Mi
1.
2.

Goodbye Song

(It's Time to Say Goodbye)

Use with page 48 and at the end of every lesson.

At the end of each lesson, Beethoven Bear and Mozart Mouse sing this song as they wave goodbye to all their music friends.

Sing the *Goodbye Song* as you end each music lesson.

Christine H. Barden